Millionaire Mindset for Real Estate Wealth

Traci Gagnon

Books Boost Business

Books Boost Business is part of Forever Family Forever Free group of Companies whose address can be found at BooksBoostBusiness.com.

First published in the USA
Copyright © 2021 by Traci Gagnon

First published 2021: Books Boost Business
Book: Millionaire mindset for real estate wealth – Traci Gagnon
ISBN-13: 978-1-913501-28-0

Contents

Introduction

My wonderful Realtor Family,

Have you ever looked in the mirror and said, "I thought I'd be further along by now?"

I'm Traci, and I help Realtors get financially free by mastering their mindset.

Everything has changed. Realtors with a decade of experience are getting their clocks cleaned by twenty somethings with a flashy Instagram page.

It seems like 95% of the deals are getting done by 5% of the 'local celebrity 'agents who have marketing budgets bigger than *The Kardashians.*

How can an experienced agent compete?

Over my quarter of a century in the industry, I've seen agent after agent throw money down the drain on one gimmick system after another or spend their airline miles flying to some guru of the month's "high level mastermind." And I've been one of them.

I've spent tens of thousands of dollars looking for the 'magic bullet to magically attract clients.'

Do you believe how stupid I was?

The biggest mistake Realtors make is investing in 'systems and gimmicks 'before they have their mindset mastered. Want a shortcut?

If so, you're in the right place. Probably.
If the title sparked your soul or the cover called your name, then I'm here to deliver and add massive value to you.

You see, I've been there.

On top – owning the fourth-largest Century 21 office in the US.

On bottom – blindsided, broken-hearted and broke.

On top – selling my business six weeks before the crash in 2007.

On bottom – investing my time, energy and reputation in a network marketing business for over a year only to have spent more money than I made.

On top – being the top recruiter globally for a KW.

On bottom – having to go back to selling homes because the profit share wasn't enough to cover a fraction of my overhead.

I was so afraid I was going to be on that Realtor hamster wheel forever:

- Spend the Money
- Get the Listing
- Sell the Listing
- Make the Money
- Spend the Money
- Get the Listing
- Sell the Listing
- Make the Money
- Spend the Money

Sound familiar? Then we are kindred spirits.

But I did do one thing right.

I went all in with Mastering My Mindset.
And it's paid off. Big.

Today, I make over a Million a Year and work less than ten hours a week.

I'm engaged to the kindest soul I've ever met, who also has time and money freedom.

We have two stunning homes and a beautiful family, and have more fun than the guys in *Animal House*.

And it all came from a small shift in Mindset and taking the right action at the right time.

And I can help you get there. Quickly.

This short, powerful book will put you on the right path.

Who this book is for:

If you're a Realtor, or considering the profession, and you want to do as Stephen Covey said and "Begin with the end in mind," this book will set you on that course. If you are committed to doing the right things in the right order and NOT getting distracted with every Facebook post promising 'social media miracles, 'you've found your guide.

Who this book is not for:

Egomaniacs. In fact, you'll hate me.

Agents who 'love their broker 'or 'don't want to make a change ' more than they love Financial Peace. You're gonna have to put your needs and your loved ones 'economic security above your need for 'more of the same. 'You absolutely must align yourself with a brokerage & team obsessed with your success.

Most Realtors have an inflated idea about their future self. Let me prove it to you by asking you a few simple questions.

How long have you been working (including babysitting and mowing lawns)?

_____ Years

How many years could you live off your investments and residual income if you could no longer work? Or better yet, if you decided you didn't want to?

_____ Years? Months? Weeks?

Did you think you'd be further ahead by now?

Want some tough love? If you've been working more than 20 years, and you're still not free, and you stay where you are in your career, and you don't master your mindset, you are probably not going to be free in another two decades.

Because if you always do what you've always done, you'll always get what you've always gotten.

And, tragically, for most Realtors, they are in Pain.

This Short Book is the ShortCut.

It will show you how to free your soul.

And you can do it. These pages will show you the way.

Thank you for letting me be your coach. I take that responsibility very seriously.

Please connect with me on Social Media!

Instagram - **TraciLewis.Realtor**
YouTube - **eXplode Your Real Estate Career**
Facebook - **Millionaire Mindset For Real Estate Wealth** LinkedIn - **Traci (Gero) Lewis.**

I'm looking forward to meeting you at one of my many live events, and I promise to deliver massive value and serve you with Love.

Traci

CHAPTER ONE
Mind Control

The mind is the ultimate enigma. It baffles the best-trained neurosurgeons and the most expensive psychiatrists. There is no way to grasp its capacity or delicateness. When your mind is stimulated, you can create the next modern miracle or produce a Hollywood blockbuster. When it's damaged, you can't even open your eyes.

What separates the ultra-successful high school dropouts from those who graduate top in their MBA class but never manage to make six figures? How they make their minds work for them. It's not education or connections. It's putting your ultimate power to work while you focus on the highest and best use of your time.

This short, powerful book will show you the steps. The only question is: Are you ready for the dramatic effect it's going to have on every part of your life?

The Conscious and the Subconscious

It's so tempting to try to break the mind up into the conscious and the subconscious, since it makes things easier to understand. The only catch is that the two are impossible to separate. The conscious mind controls your actions. It makes the decisions and puts your foot on the gas. The subconscious mind provides the mental focus and the power necessary to make it all happen.

Let's apply this to an example from real life. Say your love spends a little too long ogling the wait staff. You respond by getting irritated and telling him you find it rude of him to stare at the staff's assets while on a date with you. He'll grovel and tell you you're the only one, but your subconscious may have already filed away "I'm not sexy enough" or "He's looking for someone else." Even if your date does all the right things to make it right, it's too late. You've already lost the inner battle and your toxicity will grow.

You can't control your date's eye movements. All you can control in life is how you react to each event. How does your mind choose to respond? Guard this carefully because it controls every part of your persona. You get what you think about, whether you want it or not.

Your Persona

Your persona, the very essence of who you are, is a direct result of how you've chosen to respond to the day-to-day stimuli of your life. Everything you express through your persona comes from reactions to things that have happened to you – not from what actually happened to you. The conscious mind experiences an event. The subconscious processes what it means. Does your lover eyeing another mean he isn't that into you, or does it mean he's sexually charged from being in your presence? This difference in perspective shows why it's imperative to control your reactions and your emotions.

My mentor, Tony Robbins, talks extensively about being in a "Beautiful State." This is truly the most powerful concept to embrace. Ultimately, the only thing we truly control is our state of mind. What we focus on. How we feel. How we react. Every other freedom can be taken away. But this alone is exclusively under our control.

The subconscious mind is fertile, taking in every event in your life, so it's important to feed it excellent intentions and positive responses. Every single reaction will take root. While you can always weed out negative thoughts, it's exhausting work. Focus on the best and most uplifting thoughts, and your life will flow more smoothly.

Any idea that you consider important or any desire that burns within you will impress itself on your subconscious and reproduce tenfold. These ideas and desires manifest themselves as your persona and make up who you are. That means you can alter your personal self. The subconscious mind obeys your conscious decisions, so anything you desire is achievable if you impact it strongly enough on your subconscious. This is the power of Your Great Within.

Change Your Thoughts, Change Your Life

Every choice you make either confirms who you are or changes who you are, so there are no small decisions. Change starts with quiet discontent. You begin to hear a small voice inside that gnaws away at you: "There has to be something more." Most people learn how to tune it out, stay where they are and be 'thankful that they have it better than others. 'And it's so easy to do – just turn on the radio and suddenly you're in the thoughts of Beyoncé. Pop on social media and you're in the thoughts of your cousin. Or even worse, watch the news, and you're in the thoughts of someone who paid millions to program you. This is tragic. Within each of us lies the power to transform who we are and the ability to reinvent our life. That's the good news. The flip side is that it's going to cost you ... and the initial investment is pretty high. But nothing, NOTHING, is worse than lying to yourself about your desire for a different, better life. Especially, since you have the ability to achieve it. I can tell you from personal experience that the payoff will exceed anything you can imagine now – not just the financial rewards, but the lifestyle you'll create for yourself and the people you love.

The secret to designing the life of your dreams is in harnessing the power of your mind.

Burn Your Boat

Hernando Cortez understood the power of not having any other options. When he and his army arrived in Veracruz, Mexico, he came up with a brilliant way of making sure his men were as committed to conquering this new land as he was. He burned all their boats! By removing the option of retreat, their victory was assured. It was a bold move but it secured their success. Moreover, Cortez became a legend.

As the leader of one of the largest Revenue Share groups in my company, eXp Realty, I've seen agent after agent hold onto their 'real job 'while they dabble in Real Estate. LUNACY! They do both jobs poorly and, after a few months, their current employer thinks they're lazy and their family thinks they've abandoned them. They still haven't sold a house and they assume they aren't any good at Real Estate. Tragically, they give up their passion when they are just inches away from victory. They return to the life they hated, feeling demoralized and worse than when they started.

All the tools an agent needs to succeed are a few clicks and a few hours of focus on income-producing activities. The reason most fail is simple. They have not mastered their mindset.

We all have great inner power. The power is self-faith. There's really an attitude to winning. You have to see yourself winning before you win. And you have to be hungry. You have to want to conquer.

> *"Everybody pities the weak.*
>
> *Jealousy you have to earn."*
>
> —*Arnold Schwarzenegger*

If you're going to change your life, then you must burn your boat. It is almost impossible to be wildly successful at something new while you're holding on to something you want to leave. You have to impress upon your subconscious just how strongly you *intend* to succeed and that means leaving the safety net behind!

Desire

The origin of the word 'Desire 'is Latin, and it means 'of the spirit. ' When you desire something, it literally means it comes from your higher power, your higher source, your deepest essence.

Nothing is more powerful than desire. You must be clear about what you really want out of life and fervently focus on it. Teach yourself to expand on your dreams and believe that life can be any way you want it. Desire provides a foundation while you build on these dreams.

"Champions aren't made in gyms. Champions are made from something they have deep inside them – a desire, a dream, a vision. They have to have last-minute stamina, they have to be a little faster, they have to have the skill and the will. But the will must be stronger than the skill."

—Muhammad Ali

Know Your Goals

In 1979, researchers interviewed graduates from the Harvard MBA Program and found that:
84% had no specific goals at all
13% had goals but they were not committed to paper
3% had clear, written goals and plans to accomplish them.
In 1989, those same students were interviewed. The results were staggering.
The 13% of the class who had goals were earning, on average, twice as much as the 84% who had no goals at all.
Even more staggering – the 3% who had clear, written goals were earning, on average, ten times as much as the other 97% put together.

Figuring out your goals forces you to sit down, plan out what it is you want and expand on it. You have to understand where you want to go before you can make any strides to get there. Until you know your goal, you're moving in circles. It's like playing a game of chess but not knowing any of the rules. You'd just be moving pieces around.

I used to have over 1,000 goals. Now I've refined it to six. And all of them can be summed up in this simple statement:

*"I Am Living Peacefully and Prosperously
in a Beautiful State."*

The reason my goal list has shrunk is because I've accomplished many of the goals I set in the past 25 years. That's a powerful place to be – and I'm grateful that BECAUSE I had goals, they came to fruition. And I'm having a magnificent life – one I designed.

Sometimes, new goals are forced upon us. In April of 2000, Tiger Woods told the *NY Times*, "The only way I know is to be yourself, and to understand what you want to accomplish in life. What do you really want? You have to answer that question. And I know what I really want. I want to be the best player who ever lived."

For the record, Tiger has the lowest scoring average of a player in the history of the PGA tour. Mission accomplished.

In May of 2021, a few weeks after his horrific car accident, Tiger told ESPN that his number one goal is to be able to walk on his own. He declined to answer about whether he hoped to play golf again.

Goals change.

Most people don't think past the end of the day or the beginning of the weekend unless they're arranging a vacation. That's when the planning gene seems to kick in! That's a mistake. Planning your goals is necessary both in everyday duties and long-term achievements.

Think of everything you'd like to accomplish – there should be hundreds of things. Then narrow these down to what you want in the next week, month, year, seven years and, ultimately, how you want to live when time and money are no longer an issue. Revisit your goals at least every quarter – mostly so you can see all the progress you've made.

Just remember you can have Anything you want, but you can't have Everything you want. Focus on what brings you the most happiness and peace, and the universe will open doors at Warp Speed.

Star In Your Own Screenplay

Spend an hour writing the screenplay for your bold new life. What is the backdrop? What time do you get out of bed in the morning? This is a bigger step than you can imagine. Chances are, in your dream life, you don't have any desire to hit the snooze button. So what comes next? What's the first thing you do when you wake up? Have sex? Hit the gym? Meditate? Linger over a very expensive coffee? Call someone you adore?

How does your new life look? How does it feel? What do you do for money? Fun? Romance? How do you show your friends that you support them? How many people will you help today? Know exactly what you want and build on the vision of how you want your life to be. Then develop a plan and direct your subconscious.

And finally take Action!

"Success is dependent on effort."

—Sophocles

If you engage your mind and your effort, the strength you have inside will flow outward. Your actions will bring you closer to your goals, and your passion for life and love will grow. Picture your new life in your mind. Relish it. Plan ways to achieve it. Then take the step only a few will take. Act on it. Do it now! Don't even wait until you're finished reading this book to set out on your way.

Your first action can be as simple as writing a rough outline of your new venture or calling someone you love to tell them how important they are to you. Maybe it's a much grander step, like quitting your job or writing the intro to your first book. Or saying "I Love You" *to yourself.*

Whatever it is, now is the time to start.

Empowering Yourself

As you're empowering your mind, you'll find that it is pure bliss to mentally design the world you want. But desire without action is wasted. Having a dream that you don't attempt to achieve is worse than having no dreams at all. We all wish for second chances in life. Give yourself one.

Nature Abhors A Vacuum

My single friends often complain about the lack of datable folks. But let's be honest – if you are sitting next to Mr. Wrong, there is no place for Mr. Right. Many folks hang on to what's not working 'until something better comes along. 'This is pure rubbish. Quite often the universe will intervene – sometimes at the most inconvenient times. If you're miserable in your job and you really want to do real estate full time, the universe may, in order to help you along, make that job ... disappear. The same thing happens in many relationships.

As with every other part of life, it's so much better to be extremely proactive and take Massive Action whenever something is not working. Nature abhors a vacuum. Use that to your advantage and it can be a shortcut to the life that you've always dreamed of.

"If you don't pay attention to the problem, the
pebble then becomes like a brick. The brick
upside your head is a crisis. If you don't pay
attention to the brick upside your head, the
crisis turns into a disaster and the whole house
– brick wall – comes falling down."

—*Oprah Winfrey*

Know your Numbers

As a Realtor, your ability to stay in the game often comes down to cash flow. If you know your numbers you are light years ahead and a step closer to financial freedom.

You can't save your way into abundance. You have to understand leverage and make your money work harder than you do.

The best money is residual money. I worked every hour of the day until eXp set me free because of their ground breaking revenue share program. As Warren Buffett said "If you don't find a way to make money while you sleep, you will work until you die."

There are 6 numbers every Realtor should know:

1. Your credit score - and do all you can to get it to 850! My friend Kendra Pack helped me go from a credit score so low I couldn't get a credit card to obtaining an American Express Platinum card!
2. Your debt-to-income ratio. This will give you a much more accurate picture of how indebted you are rather than just looking at your total debt balance alone.
3. Your monthly expenses - go back a year and really dig down on what you spent and why.
4. Your Savings rate.
5. Your investment rate.
6. Your net worth (this is the Fun One!)

My friend and fellow Tony Robbins inner circle member, Laura Helen Herbert, made the decision to live a life of total time and money freedom and travels the world full time with her beautiful family. She developed a simple tool to help you know your numbers and offered to share it with my readers.

"Money is a terrible master but an excellent servant."

P.T. Barnum

KNOW YOUR NUMBERS

INCOME 1	INCOME 2	OTHER INCOME	TOTAL INCOME

FIXED EXPENSES	BUDGETED	ACTUAL		VARIABLE EXPENSES	BUDGETED	ACTUAL

DEBT/SAVINGS	BUDGETED	ACTUAL			BUDGETED	ACTUAL
				TOTAL INCOME		
				FIXED EXPENSES —		
				VARIABLE EXPENSES		
				DEBT/SAVINGS —		
				TOTAL LEFTOVER		

A free download form that you can input your own numbers in is available at

www.foreverfamilyforeverfree.com/know-your-numbers-worksheet

CHAPTER TWO
Change Your Mind

You should have heard the disbelief in her voice when I decided to change my life. "How could you leave teaching?! It's such a great job! And you get summers off! And you get paid so much! And you'll be wasting your college education!"

From my mom's perspective, this was absolutely true. I made more in my first year teaching than she had ever made as a secretary. But I knew there were women out there my age making ten times more than me, and I was smarter and more driven than most of them. I knew I wanted to do more than just get a higher salary than my parents did. I wanted to have it all! I was ready to trade security for my dreams of success.

There will always be someone to tell you "no." You decide if they are right.

"We don't like their sound and guitar music is on the way out."

—Decca Recording Co., 1962

(upon rejecting the Beatles) $$$$

Stop Trying

All your dreams, goals and visions start between the ears. I tried to leave teaching after my second year – really tried! (Yes, and I heard Yoda inside my head. And he was right). I got a job in sales and had every intention of squeaking out a living. And I got to wear cooler clothes! But I chose a job in which most people fail and very few make over six figures. To make matters worse, the office was like *Peyton Place* and I wasn't savvy enough to navigate those waters.

After two months, I was back in the classroom, licking my wounds. I had failed. I decided I really was a school teacher after all. The only problem was that my eyes had been opened. I'd experienced the professional life that I dreamed of, and had a taste of business travel and nice lunches. I'd been ruined forever for the school cafeteria! I glimpsed what was beyond the walls of my own making. That's the way to discover what you really want to do. Taste the world outside your comfort zone and find out what exhilarates your soul.

Three years later, in a heartbeat, everything changed. This time the change came from within. That made all the difference.

When I finally fully decided that I needed to change my life, I acted quickly and burned my boat. If I failed I couldn't go back, so failure meant more uncertainty and I fought against that. In the profound (profane?) words of Eminem, "Success was my only *$!&A&@# option."

Success comes slowly at first, then strikes at the speed of lightning. But it all starts with a firm decision. It's not enough to say, "I'll give it a try." In fact, remove that word from your vocabulary. Don't ever 'try 'anything again. 'Do. 'Decide you must be an outrageous success. Decide you won't live another day complacent with the way things are. Decide that you deserve so much more. Then demand it from yourself.

"Do or do not. There is no try."

Yoda

Your Personal Concierge

The subconscious mind obeys, absolutely, the desires of your conscious mind. The only limits placed on it are by you. This is Your Great Within, the ultimate concierge, which will bring wonderful things into your life. But it's not as easy as room service, where everything is just brought to your door. You have to create it for yourself by directing your subconscious to go after your desires.

Unlimited possibilities exist in the subconscious of every mind. To believe this is freedom personified. Know what you want to achieve, know you can achieve it and doubts disappear completely. You're free to succeed!

You first have to decide exactly what you want to impress upon your subconscious mind. More importantly, you must feel the soul of the idea. If you feel your desires with a deep, strong passion, they will penetrate your subconscious and spark it into action. But you can't simply command it to happen. You must want it enough to make it real.

Don't just tell yourself you want to be rich. Who doesn't want to be rich? Let it sink into your subconscious exactly how you want to feel and what you want to experience. Internalize the details of the decor in that second home you want on the beach and how it will feel with your toes in the sand and your love beside you. Focus on these 'Beach Thoughts 'all the time and they will become tangible and within reach. Think that's pleasurable? Wait 'til you feel the real thing.

"I've had the same goal I've had ever since I was a girl. I want to rule the world. I'm tough, ambitious and I know exactly what I want. Poor is the person whose pleasures depend on the permission of another."

Madonna

Trust Yourself

Believe in your abilities. Follow your role models who have shown it can be done, or get some new ones.

There are no limits. Saying you want to be as successful as Jeff Bezos puts a cap on things. Don't think about doing better today than you did yesterday. That gives the subconscious two antagonistic ideas (the lesser achievements of the past and the greater achievements of the future). Think only about your awesome achievements. Better ones will follow.

Focus on your successes, and outsource things you don't enjoy and don't do well. Thinking about past failures can only create more failures. Everything is different now. This time, you know you have the power within you.

Know who you want to become, and resolve to become that soul.

Passion Doesn't Need Permission

Remember that this is your life and no one else's. Any time you decide to make changes, there will be people you care about who will try to talk you out of it. Some of them are well-meaning but passive (they'll say "practical"). Or maybe they just don't want you to outgrow them. But their motives are irrelevant. Don't waste time trying to figure them out. If you know what you're doing is right and makes sense for you, then live your passion. Your family will find a whole new level of support for you when they're snorkeling in Maui.

CHAPTER THREE
Develop A Plan Of Attack

There is an ancient Zen story about a young man who started a voyage of 1,000 miles. The beginning of his journey was on the water, so he constructed a very good boat. That boat served him well for the first part of his adventure, so when he came to land, he decided it would be wrong just to leave something behind that had gotten him so far. So he carried the boat with him. And he never made it to the end of his voyage.

Release Your Fears

Take an inventory of what you're holding on to. Relationships you've outgrown. Negative ways of seeing yourself. Something as simple as the clothes in your closet. Anything not propelling you toward a better tomorrow should be released. You're going to need a whole new skill set for your new life and there simply isn't room in your carry-on bag to bring unnecessary items. Lose them. Now that packing is out of the way, let's plan an itinerary. If you knew you couldn't fail, how would you spend the next five years? Find a pen and actually WRITE the answers. There is something we don't understand about putting pen to paper — remember the Harvard Goal Setting study we talked about?

_____

_____

_____

_____

_____

_____

It's vital to answer that question! If you get in touch with what you most enjoy, it's easy to figure out how to build your work around that. Really consider every aspect of your dream job, from the lifestyle to the paycheck. Remember that you can find ways to make a fortune doing anything. Martha Stewart is the ultimate example. She built a billion-dollar industry based on homemaking. Take what you love and make it turn a profit.

Do Your Homework

Learn everything you can about the different ways to make money in your Real Estate Career. eXp has multiple ways of helping Realtors make money - that's a big part of why it's the fastest growing real estate company in the US. Really dive into whatever you can get your hands on to discover the lifestyle, the income potential and the people who thrive in the industry.

I chose Real Estate because it made sense to me to sell a high-priced item without paying for inventory or overhead. People warned me that it was hard work and that most agents failed in their first year, but I knew my abilities, and I went into it with my eyes open and my boat burned. The first company that recruited me offered a 50/50 split between agent and broker. At first, I felt obligated to join them since they encouraged me early on. Then one of my instructors at Real Estate school reminded me that my first obligation was to myself. Awesome advice!! I did my homework and found an agency that offered 70/30 splits, plus it had some of the most successful agents in the industry.

Add that financial opportunity to my passion for houses and it was a no-brainer. (Actually, it was a 'full-brainer – 'a conscious decision impressed on the subconscious mind.)

For five months, I didn't earn anything. Then in my sixth month, I made $12,000 – about half of what I made all year as a teacher. I finished that year making over two and a half times what I earned the year before! Plus, I got to go to the bathroom without waiting for the bell to ring!

When I was introduced to eXp, I cried. I wasn't particularly happy with my current real estate company; however, I was making lots of money and was in a really nice rhythm. But when I saw eXp and the power of the additional revenue streams, I knew that it would be financially irresponsible for me to not join this groundbreaking company. It forced me out of my comfort zone, but for the first time in my life, I was making a decision based on moving toward pleasure instead of away from pain, and that was a huge game-changer for me.

eXp offers something that no other company in our industry does – the opportunity to build massive residual income. I made over $1,000,000 in 2020 and worked less than ten hours a week on average. In addition to that, the company encourages us to buy our personal investment properties, growing our wealth that way, and offers, in my humble opinion, the best commission structure in the industry. You can learn more about this life-changing company at www.ExplodeYourCareer.com.

It's not the right fit for everyone, but at the time of writing this book, it seems the best company for entrepreneur agents and brokers.

People choose real estate companies for all kinds of different reasons. However, most people join the very first company that they interview with. That's Insanity. It's too big of a decision. You should check out all the major players in the industry and a couple of the minor players before you make your final decision. The great news is that changing real estate companies is an ego risk, not a Financial Risk.

If any of you reading this book are contemplating opening up your own brokerage, please reach out to me via social media. The reason Brokers are called Brokers is because they are usually Broker Than their agents. Very, very, very few people succeed with a franchise, so if you're considering that route, do reach out to me. I can save you from a lot of Heartache and at least teach you some of the right questions to ask before you jump off that ten-year commitment ledge.

Ask The Right Questions

I'm dumbfounded that so many people dream of opening a restaurant. Statistically, four out of five new restaurants close within the first year. Yet, people still dream of owning one! Also think about the lifestyle. What hours are most restaurants open? Do you really want to work those hours? You may be thinking that you'll let someone else run it while you simply reap the rewards. Okay, then call a new restaurant in your area and ask them how dependable their staff have been.

I'm not trying to talk you out of your dream. Quite the opposite. I want you to make sure it's the right dream for you before you sign the lease.

One of the most important things to consider is the *lifestyle* that goes along with the profession – the hours, the opportunity for leverage – otherwise, you are just buying yourself a job.

Create Your Own Opportunities

Opportunities abound everywhere! Think of all the creative ways that people have made fortunes doing what they want. They didn't wait for an invitation to innovation.

Direct your mind to create an opportunity, then push yourself to put it into action. The subconscious cannot act alone – it needs a little elbow grease.

If you're struggling in Real Estate, take a look at the agents in your company. Do they have the life you crave? If not, it might be time to consider a new brokerage. Find someone who has the LIFESTYLE you want and offer to intern for them FOR FREE, if necessary, for a few hours a week! Yes, I know you have to earn a living. Find a job that will enable you to pay your bills, but will give you the flexibility to pursue your passion.

You hear me talk about lifestyle a bunch. That's because I have met so many real estate agents who make massive amounts of money, and work every hour of the day and come home to an empty house. So many agents are sick, overweight, and miserable. That's not success, no matter how much money you have in your bank. I always focused on listings and, as a result, I never worked on weekends or even Friday nights.

Then I found a new model that would allow me to work very hard for two and a half years, and now I work about ten hours a week. I'm doing a lot of the same things I was doing at Century 21 and

Keller Williams to recruit real estate agents. This model simply compensates that behavior more than the other models did. And it has set me financially free.

Stay close to your goals. Talk to the people you want to be like and ask for advice — especially about their lifestyle. Be sure it's a lifestyle you would enjoy. Picture yourself doing what they do. Realize you have the ability to get there.

And always, ALWAYS ask the folks living your dream what their exit strategy is! This is the step most folks miss when they start planning for their new life.

When people would call telling me how desperately they wanted to be a Realtor, I'd offer them a job. I'd tell them that if they'd work ten hours at my company, I'd pay for a class. Most people would tell me that sounded great and would promise to get back to me after checking their schedules. Less than 10% ever called back. Those who followed through often became my best agents because they were willing to do whatever was necessary to achieve their dreams.

Pay The Price

It is important to know that you will, in some way, have to 'pay the price.' Understand that there is a price to pay for success and a price to pay for failure. Which is your preference?

You can work dynamically and have it all, or you can just put in your time and get whatever the boss has left over. You don't have to work more hours to have more things. You do have to work differently and be willing to take huge risks. You must be ready to 'risk your security,' which is another way of saying you must be ready to throw off your shackles. Don't trade in your time and passion just for a paycheck.

The way that companies stay in business is to harness the intellectual and physical power of the people who work for them. When you get up every morning and go to your job, you are making someone else wealthy or improving their quality of life. That's very nice and generous, but not at all fair to you. If you're going to

expend the energy, why not make yourself wealthy and improve your quality of life?
Ask yourself the tough questions.

What are you holding on to? Really think about it. What are you afraid of losing if you follow your passion?

If you stay where you are right now, what will your life be like in six months?
A. It will be exactly the same.
Or
B. It will be different because _____ _____

_____

_____

_____ will change.

What will your life be like in a year?
A. It will be exactly the same.
Or
B. It will be different because _____ _____

_____

_____

_____ will change.
What kind of car will you be driving?

_____

What kind of home will you be living in?

_____

How will you spend your free time?

_____

_____

Do you feel this is good enough for you?

Yes
No

If the answer is 'no, 'then you know what's next. Risk or regret? Change your life or compromise yourself?

No Plastic Surgery Required

If you think you can, you can. If you think you can't, you're right. It's all inside you. Each person is, no more and no less, the sum total of what they believe in their subconscious. If you want to change something about yourself, the first step is to consciously direct the subconscious to correct every flaw, every defect in your personality that may be standing in your way.

Many people fail to improve because they live in constant consciousness of their imperfections. They feel they are ordinary and, consequently, they pass this signal on to their subconscious where it is realized. Rare are those people, however, who live in the ideal and think always of the greater worth that is within them.

To remove wrong images that have been impressed on your subconscious (and manifest themselves in your persona), an opposite, correct impression must take its place. Procrastinator? Picture yourself finishing before a deadline. Think of all the productive things you can accomplish in your spare time. Imagine how good it feels to get that project off your plate and your toes in the sand. Let your subconscious drink in that desire.

Negative desires can also impress themselves strongly, so don't dwell on these. Don't think, "I don't want to be broke." Instead, imagine yourself being Prosperous and Productive. The corresponding change will take place in your mind and body. A new, better version of yourself. No scalpel needed ... but you'll feel twenty years younger!

CHAPTER FOUR
Empower Your Image

We've already established that the subconscious provides the essentials necessary to achieve your dreams. It's up to you to consciously apply that vital energy to produce practical results. These are the outward expressions of your inner power and the whole world benefits!

As your subconscious responds to your deeply felt desires, it produces an irresistible urge to succeed that radiates throughout your being. You'll be propelled into action. You'll never need 'motivation 'again. You will, instead, be divinely guided.

Your Image

The way you see yourself affects every part of who you are and what you do. A big part of how you see yourself is reflected in the image you show everyone else. Image isn't everything, but it is an expression of who you are and what you're relaying to the world. That's important enough to merit serious consideration.

Who you want to be is directly connected to how people see you. So you've got to determine what image to show them. Decide exactly what kind of person you want to become. Internalize it. Impress your subconscious. Then allow it to be outwardly expressed.

Write down a description of the person you will empower yourself to become.

_____

_____

_____

Now, ask yourself how this person would dress. Are you wearing those kinds of clothes now? If not, then change! Inner change requires outward change. Let's say your goal is to be a Prosperous Realtor and help others grow as well. Think of a famous role model who you connect with and who has the lifestyle you crave. Emulate their dress, style, and attitude until you are confident in your own. When you go on a sales call or talk with your colleagues, channel that person. It really works!! Your persona gets in sync with your passions. Your actions must be consistent with this appearance and attitude. How would your role model spend a free Friday night? Think about that before you head to the cheapest happy hour in town. Focus on what you want to be. Then every other decision in your life will become much clearer.

Look the Part

When I started in Real Estate, I had huge debts and no cash. I did have a few credit cards though, so I hit the resale shops and made out like a bandit. I bought three used suits at a fraction of the value. Yes, my colleagues got tired of seeing me in the same clothes over and over, but in Real Estate, you don't see the same clients every day, so the people who were earning me a living had no idea I had a small wardrobe. Those clothes were a brilliant investment.

"Clothes make the man. Naked people have
little or no influence on society."

—*Mark Twain*

Even when I started making more money, I remembered all the tricks that had served me when I was broke. Two good pairs of pants in blue and black can get you through the winter. Just add different blouses and costume jewelry, which are a lot less expensive. Spend time in discount stores to reproduce designer looks on a budget you can afford. There are ways to look like a millionaire without spending everything you earn. And only buy one or two things at a time. We are always evolving!

They say the fit is important, so make sure your clothes fit the lifestyle you'd like to lead and the area where you live. Whether you're running to the store or heading to the gym, look sharp. You never know who you'll meet or what connections can be made! And always wear you name badge! Not only will it open doors it helps casual acquaintances remember your name.

When you go into a clothing store, find the sales person who emulates the look you want. Talk to them about the image you want to create. A good salesperson will do everything possible to guide you in the right direction and they know their inventory. After all, if they inspire you, they will make more sales on commission. Also, update your hair and all other aspects of your appearance (make-up, accessories) to reflect your professional persona.

Take Care Of Yourself

You have the body you deserve. I once heard a body builder in my gym say he'd eat a pound of dung if it would give him a pound of muscle. Now that, ladies and gentlemen, is being goal-oriented and directing your actions toward your desires.

> "The higher your energy level, the more
> efficient your body; the more efficient your
> body, the better you feel and the more you will
> use your talent to produce outstanding
> results."

> —Tony Robbins

If you want to be healthy but eat fried foods, you're lying to yourself. You don't really want to be healthy – you want to eat whatever you want to eat. Your intentions and actions are at odds and you're sending mixed signals to your subconscious, which renders it powerless. Focus on your desire to be healthy and make a conscious decision to follow through. That sends the message to every part of your being that you deserve to be healthy, and it will respond in like. You can then use your renewed energy to become more efficient in other areas of your life.

Your Car

Projecting the appropriate image goes beyond your physical self to incorporate every aspect of your life ... even your car. It's a cold, hard, ugly truth. People will judge your level of success by the car you drive.

It's more than that, though. If you want to impress upon your subconscious the desire to be successful, then you must present yourself as successful even to yourself. That doesn't mean going into debt to drive a Ferrari! The anxiety of meeting the payments will wreak havoc on your subconscious mind, sending mixed signals of success overshadowed by failure and financial doom.

Don't dwell on something you can't afford – this only creates self-destructive feelings of envy. Focus only on achieving success and make the proper, conscious decisions to ensure it. Remember, you already have it all inside of you. Believe in yourself and the Ferraris will come!

For now, this means you may need to buy a used, clean, luxury car instead of a new mid-range car. The image your car portrays is more important than words can say.

The operative word here, however, is 'clean. 'Don't surround yourself with clutter. This impresses a feeling of chaos and loss of control onto your subconscious. Also, you never know when you may need to offer a client or colleague a ride home.

A car is also a vehicle for personal growth. We all spend a big chunk of time commuting, and this can be transformed into an extremely powerful and productive part of the day. Think of your car as a rolling university and use this time to feed your mind. Turn off 'Classic Rock 'and put on Podcasts. Success is just up the road!

Invest In Yourself

I invest in the safest thing humanly possible – myself. I spend a lot of money on my education. My college degree, which cost me four years of my life and thousands of dollars, got me a job earning $20,000 a year. My Real Estate license took twelve days and cost me $800. It has made me wealthy. The Tony Robbins and Tom Hopkins workshops I've attended cost a few hundred dollars each. They've made me millions. Do the math!

While college is a great experience and a good opportunity, you shouldn't stop there. In many cases, you shouldn't even start there. Education is a continuing process, one that becomes more needs-specific as you narrow down your goals.

> *"Books were my pass to personal freedom. I*
> *learned to read at age three, and soon*
> *discovered there was a whole world to conquer*
> *that went beyond our farm in Mississippi."*
>
> *—Oprah Winfrey*

Jim Rohn, one of the most prolific and inspiring life coaches in the world, talks about how all the really good stuff in life is up on the top shelf and the only way we can access it is to stand on the books that we've read. What a powerful image! He also says you'll be the same next year as you are today except for the books you read and the audiotapes you listen to, the seminars you attend, and the people you hang around. Of course, not all learning is limited to literature or confined to a classroom. After all, Andrew Carnegie only had four years of formal education. Instructional books and seminars are a bargain and can help you master virtually any skill. They bring you closer to success and, best of all, personal growth is guaranteed.

Find Balance

No matter how success-driven you are and how hard you impress your subconscious with the desire to succeed, you simply cannot afford to allow your existence to only center on work. You'll start to resent work or look upon it merely as a means or duty, and your mind will pick up on these negative emotions.

> *"Not personal? That is my work, my sweat and*
> *my time away from my kids! If that's not*
> *personal, I don't know what is!"*
>
> —*Erin Brockovich*

If you find you have trouble concentrating on anything but work, then find ways to mix business with pleasure. Tom Hopkins, one of the greatest sales trainers of all time, coined the term 'PLRK 'to describe where play and work are combined. For example, join the Chamber of Commerce or the Rotary or Toastmasters – any business-minded group. It'll revolutionize your social life and you'll meet some influential and fascinating people.

Quite often, charity connections bring the biggest opportunities. Not only will they bring you personal satisfaction and altruism, but they can do wonders for your business. Bill Gates 'mother, Mary, was on the national board of the United Way. So was IBM's Chief Executive, dubbed "The Brain of IBM." It's rumored that this connection helped open doors for Bill.

In my own experience, San Antonio has eleven different Rotaries. I joined the one with the most millionaires, which also happened to be the largest one in the world. Not only did I increase my social circle by 900 people, I also get lunch, weekly speakers and the chance to talk to business people who have been successes longer than I've been eating solid food. All this for only $8.50 a week. Now, that's a cheap date!

Guard Your Free Time

You make your 'living 'from nine to five. You make your 'life 'during all the rest of the hours. Make it count! If you're not working, use your time constructively. Don't waste an hour. Invest in the people and things you care about. The sense of well-being you'll feel will impress itself upon your subconscious, equating success with happiness in all areas of your life.

If I gave you $29,200 you'd be thrilled, right? But what if that were all the money you'd ever get in your entire life? Would you spend even 50 cents on a candy bar? How careful would you be with that money? Well, the average life span in 2021 is 80 years. That's 29,200 days. Now does it seem harder to spend three hours in front of the TV? Time is your most precious commodity. Invest it wisely.

If happy hour with your colleagues is cutting into time that could be spent with family, realize the price you're paying. Success in business brings rewards and freedom for you and your family to enjoy.

Personal Success

Don't confuse financial success with personal success. I've known a whole lot of wealthy people who were miserable – unhappy in their marriages, unhappy in their friendships (if they had friends), and unhappy with what they did for a living. Some felt that they'd sold their soul to afford a nice house. It's not worth it! Success is about finding what it is that brings you peace and joy, and allows you to live in a state of utter bliss.

That also means making peace with every single person – if you don't, you'll live with a nagging sense of unrest. From your end, there should be nothing but love and forgiveness in your heart.

Family

It's important to feel your passions deeply, not fleetingly. This requires the ability to really live in the moment. When you're home, BE home. Thinking about a difficult client while you're eating dinner with your family doesn't help anyone – not the client, not the kids, not your appetite. It's holding on to things from the past (albeit, the recent past) that can't propel you into the present. Your personal life is precious. Without a feeling of personal satisfaction and connection, success is usually hollow.

Old Friends

The people you care about won't always join you on your journey. As your success grows, you grow. That may mean you'll outgrow some of the things you used to enjoy or find inspiring. This is a shift in paradigm and doesn't reflect badly on your friends. Remember, you are the one changing, not them.

> "Old friends pass away, new friends appear. It is just like the days. An old day passes a new day arrives. The important thing is to make it meaningful - a meaningful friend - or a meaningful day. "
>
> — Dalai Lama

As you continue to change into the person you want to be, you may need to make new friends, see fresh perspectives, discuss different ideas. This is not to say you should sever ties with old and dear friends. It just means that you shouldn't be surprised if some of them stay behind as you expand your horizons.

I was raised in Texas, where my business first started to thrive. Initially, I was dumbfounded by the number of people I knew who first tried to downplay, then attack, my success. I assumed the people in my life would be thrilled for me ... call me Pollyanna!

Victor Rueda, one of my agents and a gentleman in every sense of the word, told me a story that put it in perspective. When he was a young boy, he and his dad were on the beach and came across a fisherman carrying crabs in an open bucket. Victor asked the fisherman if he was worried about the crabs escaping. The old man said he wasn't the least concerned, because if one crab tried to climb out, the others would pull him right back down. Victor assured me that, in life, many people were just like those crabs and, ultimately, it was my choice if I let them keep me in that prison.

I made a conscious decision not to let other people's jealousies or insecurities interfere with my goals. I would *Defy the Odds* and design my own destiny.

CHAPTER FIVE
Personify Professionalism

Image means nothing in business without professionalism to back it up. As you focus on and work toward your dreams of becoming a huge success, make sure to act the part when you connect with people. Conduct yourself as if you already run an empire!

Professional Phone Courtesy

As you impress your desire for success onto your subconscious, it doesn't hurt to impress others with it as well. When you're talking on the phone, treat the person with the exact same courtesy you would if you were face-to-face. If you're multitasking, they will know! There's no way to disguise a lack of attention. Also, don't rush people off the phone. We all get in a hurry, but your clients must feel that they are important and the only person you are talking to today. If the conversation is taking a bad turn or rambling on, try a soft approach: "I understand what you are saying and your concerns. Let me get to work on these issues right away. Thanks for your business and I'll keep you posted."

Cell phones are our lifeblood and many of us conduct run our business & much of our life with this every changing technology. The only catch is that the quality is rarely as good as it is with a landline, so it's easy to come off a little harsher when you can't be fully heard. Control your voice and tone to match the person on the other end as closely as possible. This will make them feel like you're on the same page and will build a fast rapport.

Your voice message also says a lot. You must convey warmth, enthusiasm, and kindness, which is a delicate balance that's going to take some practice to nail. Write the message down, memorize it and stand up when you're recording it. Then ask the toughest critic in your circle to listen and evaluate it. Revamp it. Then ask the most successful person you know to review it as well. When I call someone and they have the prerecorded message my enthusiasm for talking to them... diminishes.

The Power of Words

The words you choose in everyday life also constitute a massive part of your success. Eradicate terms like "I can't" from your vocabulary. You can – you have the inner resources. Even "I don't have the time" is erroneous. We all have the same 24 hours in each day. It's how we choose to invest our time that makes the difference.

Furthermore, don't waste your breath complaining. It reinforces negative thoughts into your subconscious, does nothing to rectify the situation at hand and gives others a bad impression of you. Also, quite frankly, it's boring. The only person who wants to hear about your troubles is your therapist – and she's getting paid for it!

The power of words is derived from their meanings and a word like 'prosperity 'is a lot like 'love. 'It means something different to each individual. That's why it's important to impress upon your subconscious the entire implication of what you desire. Do you just want 'prosperity 'or do you want to live it in its truest, original sense (from Latin, meaning 'in the flow')? A prosperous life has less to do with money and more to do with peaceful, joyous, harmonious living which flows to every aspect of your existence. To be wealthy and miserable has no merit. So it's imperative to discover ways to earn a fortune doing something you're passionate about.

The Power of Images

Communicating and thinking in images is powerful beyond words. Sometimes in business, you have a vision that needs to be shared with others. If you can't make them understand, make them SEE. When George Lucas was desperately shopping *Star Wars* around to the studios, he was rejected by both Universal and United Artists.

Before talking to 20th Century Fox, he hired an artist to give life to the images in his head. Once the studio could see his vision, they gave him the green light – and $8,000,000! Mr. Lucas was fine with that budget, but he just asked for a big percentage of the merchandising. The studio didn't see much value there, so they conceded. In 2005, Lucas was worth $3 Billion. In 2021, he was worth up to $7.1 Billion.

Demand the Best

You expect the best from yourself. If you are truly devoted to succeeding, your actions must correspond to your desires so that the conscious is symbiotic with the subconscious.

When you hire other people, it gets a lot trickier. Their goals may not exactly match yours. That's why it's essential to communicate your expectations.

When you hire someone, you must demand that they bring their 'A 'game with them every day. The first time they lose their focus, remind them, kindly but firmly, that you depend on them to always play at their highest level. If it happens again, remind them in writing and have them sign a copy. Start a paper trail. Not only will this serve you well if you have to fire them down the road, but it will prove to your employees that you are serious about holding them accountable for their work. Otherwise, they impede the progress your company could be making.

I've hired hundreds of people. I've only had to fire a handful. Even if it seems to end on good terms and you give them a nice severance package, expect repercussions, hurt feelings, or a letter from their lawyer. Donald Trump said whenever you fire someone, they will hate your guts. Remember, you're not running for prom queen. Don't lose sight of the fact that it's your job to create an environment where you and your employees can prosper. Some people just aren't on the same page. Be slow to hire, quick to fire.

If your desire for success extends to your employees, they will be exemplary at their jobs and the news will travel fast to clients and competitors. Don't be surprised if another company tries to lead them into temptation after you've invested an exorbitant amount of time and energy getting them trained and productive. Take it as a compliment to your expertise. On occasion, some people will leave. After all, while you're focusing on your goals, your employees are also doing what they feel is best for themselves. Losing even your most valued employee doesn't affect the company's ability to thrive. If they want to go, wish them well and change the locks once they leave!

One of the most powerful benefits of eXp is that we all have a vested interest in our agents growing and prospering. When I owned my Century 21 franchise, pretty much every agent who I promoted to a manager soon went and opened up their own office or went to work for a competing broker. I was always heartbroken. In retrospect, those agents were simply living the best life that they could, and we all have a deep desire to grow and build. With eXp, I want to train my agents to go out and start their own teams, since almost everybody stays with the company, and their success creates residual income for me even when they are no longer working directly for my team. It is the ultimate win-win. Join a company that promotes agents growing and prospering, and serve your fellow agents with love.

Choosing Partners

When I started making serious money, I wasn't prepared for the number of people who suddenly found me very interesting and the investment opportunities they had for me. I was flattered and took the bait. But, for the record, I rarely made a single dime off them. Until I changed my mindset about money and investing.

Choosing the right partner is even more difficult than hiring employees. It's hard to find someone who shares your vision and equals your level of commitment. I mean, most of us aren't consistently on the same page as our significant other, so why do we think we could mesh our talents and bank accounts with a virtual stranger?

I've become much more selective about who I join forces with. I now put definitive rules for partnerships in writing and, no matter how amazing the person or deal seems, I never deviate from these at all. It's imperative that they have skills and talents that complement mine, and an impressive track record. This simple rule serves me well!

It's a lot easier to find people to support your desires and help you reach them than to fit into another person's scheme, no matter how attractive or close to completion it seems. This goes back to knowing exactly what you want and not conforming to someone else's vision, which is their dream – not yours. There's a real power in staying your course. It forces you to evaluate your own strengths and weaknesses before bringing someone else in on your plan.

"Nothing interferes with my concentration.
You could put on an orgy in my office and I
wouldn't look up. Well, maybe once."

—Isaac Asimo

CHAPTER SIX
Seize the Moment

Opportunity is a mystery. Rocks don't look like much of an opportunity ... but tell that to the guy who made them pets!

Here's where most people get confused. Opportunity doesn't really knock. It doesn't even whisper. It's created. Opportunities are everywhere!

Literally, everything you see, feel, and touch has inspired opportunity in someone. Nothing is too ridiculous or outlandish. In fact, I believe that if the idea isn't a little bit out there, it's probably not very inspired.

> *"Opportunities multiply as they are seized."*
>
> —*Sun Tzu*

Turn On Your Radar

Creating opportunities is an art and a science. Like improving one's golf game or lovemaking, it takes practice and fine-tuning, so you should always have your radar on. Be open to that quiet, small spark of imagination, and remember that there is no such thing as an accident. Sometimes the right person sits next to you on an airplane or you get stuck in line and providence steps in. However it happens, when an idea inspires you, seize the moment. Never be a victim of the law of diminishing intent!

The mind is similar to a the video recorder on your phone. Under certain conditions, it can record or reproduce anything. The big difference is that it can take those ideas and make them grow exponentially. It can form, create, develop, and express whatever you desire. Utilize all of the mind's functions and focus them on unlimited opportunities. When the ideas come, put them into action!

> *"Those who dream by day are cognizant of many things which escape those who dream only by night."*
>
> —*Edgar Allan Poe*

You're Younger Than You Think

It's never too late to begin living your dreams. In the year 1900, the average life expectancy was 47 years. In 2004, it was 76. In 2021, is 80 years. If life spans continue increasing at this rate, most of us can expect to live to be well over 100. That means you may want to rethink that retirement! Use the wisdom, business savvy, and experience you have acquired over all these years and put them to work for you.

Quite often when a person has been in the same job for fifteen or twenty years, they have some regrets but figure they should stick it out. That's crazy! You may have a lot more time than you think and countless opportunities.

Colonel Sanders was well into his sixties when he decided to start his new business venture. Mary Kay was retired when she began her own cosmetics company. Both of these people spent their golden years building business empires and enjoying every single day. That's quite a different image than game shows and early-bird specials.

> *"The first person to live to be 1,000 is already alive today."*
>
> — *Aubrey de Grey*
>
> *one of the world s leading – and most talked-about – biomedical gerontologists*

What If You Had To?

Is it possible to completely eliminate our dependence on oil? The initial answer is, "Of course not." Now, let me rephrase the question. What if you absolutely, positively had to find a substitute for oil? See, your brain changes gears! If we had no way to get our hands on another drop of oil, other possibilities would flood the mind. I'm trying to get you to think of every possible outlandish plan for creating opportunities.

Any time you feel a project can't be done, reframe the question to "What if I had to?" and impress your mind to come up with new and creative ideas. In this way, you train your mind to always search for the best possible way to solve any difficult problem.

Focus on the outcome that you want instead of the problem that faces you. There is a solution. It's simply a matter of finding the right option for whatever you're up against.

Express Yourself

Envision perfect clarity and lucidity in your conscious mind. It will impress your subconscious into finding new and exhilarating ways to bring value to your work and streamline your goals.

Your subconscious has the material to produce ideas, plans, methods, and systems, but your conscious mind arranges them in a way that gets results. It's not just a matter of producing first-class work. It's the way that work is presented that opens the doors to opportunity and determines the measure of success. Proper expression equals powerful impact.

Live Without Limits

Creating your own opportunities means erasing the limits you have placed on yourself and your subconscious. Once you tap into your potential, the dreams you had five years ago will seem elementary. The life you'll be leading five years from now is going to exceed any dreams you have today.

Be open to long-term, unlimited success just as you are open to the more immediate opportunities around you. The two are a powerful combination.

Go Straight To The Top

Because opportunity won't always knock, it will sometimes be necessary for you to go knocking. Find the very best people in the industries that support or are related to yours, then get to know them. Ask them to lunch and find out all you can about their professional and personal habits for success. This will create synergy and opportunities for collaboration.

People judge you by who you do business with. Surround yourself with the best and the brightest, and watch your influence grow.

Making Sleep Work For You

When we go to sleep, all the thoughts, desires, intentions, tendencies, feelings, and ideas that have formed during the day are taken into the subconscious and will ultimately show up in your personality. Therefore, we have to eliminate all undesirable thoughts and feelings before we go to sleep. Thoroughly cleanse your conscious mind of everything you don't want to reproduce and multiply. It's a lot like cleansing your face before bed so that your skin looks radiant in the morning.

While you're sleeping, you can cultivate anything you want in your life since whatever is impressed upon the subconscious takes root in Your Great Within — the ultimate resource. Give your subconscious a definite direction about what should be reproduced and expressed. Impress upon it what you want to accomplish in the future and give it a deadline. This lets your subconscious work out the best plan, method, and ideas. You'll develop new insights, understanding, and power to supercharge your results.

The stronger our desire for wisdom, power, love, and achievements while we are awake, the more our subconscious will work for those things while we sleep. If we instead focus on pain and disappointments, it has no directive other than to produce more of the same. Weeds are harder to kill than flowers, so plant only good seeds, and delete negative thoughts and feelings before resting your body and soul. And for the love of salsa, don't watch the news. Ever.

Putting Negative Thoughts To Rest

The average person goes to sleep every night with all sorts of thoughts racing through their mind – the good and the bad, the best and the worst. The troubles and worries of the day mix with triumphs and dreams. The subconscious, consequently, continues to work for more good things on one hand and for more troubles and worries on the other. This habit of bringing mixed thoughts to bed is the principal cause of the continuous mingling of good and bad in most people's daily lives.

> *"If you can't sleep, then get up and do something instead of lying there and worrying. It's the worry that gets you, not the loss of sleep."* —Dale Carnegie

True bliss is knowing that people can emancipate themselves from their troubles and fears by refusing, absolutely, to permit a single undesirable thought, feeling, or desire to take root in the subconscious. Clear them from your conscious mind and focus only on what you want your life to be like. Make sure your entire system is in a state of peace, harmony, and order before you go to sleep, and it will radiate outwardly each day.

Never go to sleep discouraged or thinking of failure. Fear of failure impresses the subconscious with the idea of failure and it will respond by producing conditions in the system that breed failure. Similarly, going to sleep discouraged, disappointed, or worried impresses ideas of weakness that will manifest in your personality. Instead, go to bed with strong, clear ideas of health, harmony, prosperity, and love. Your subconscious will form the catalyst and you'll see these things come to life. Your health will improve, your mind and body will have more energy, and your capacity will increase. All your talents and senses will be filled with the spirit of success, and you'll do better work than before. Best of all, you'll become more loving and more lovable.

If your mind is free of negative thoughts, it can focus on the things you want to actualize. Plus, you'll get a better night's sleep – no new mattress required.

What You Control

One of the foundations of Zen philosophy is that your resistance to what IS causes all of your heartaches. Consider the possibility that every frustration in your life is simply because you're not happy about things you have no control over.

Seems like a losing proposition, unless you like banging your head against the wall. The choice is clear. You can accept things that you can't change or you can waste time and emotion lamenting over what IS.

You have no power over other people – not your love, your kids or your clients. You can give them incentives, threaten them or leave them, but their behavior is still their choice. You do, however, have the opportunity to choose your own actions accordingly ... and that's the strongest power there is.

Disappointment, anger, and frustration with others are worthless, wasted emotions. Focus on what you want for your life and treat everyone else fairly. You should expect the best in everyone, though you certainly can't force it.

Accept that many people hate to think for themselves. For some, it's out of laziness. Others are terrified of taking personal responsibility. You can't think for them. But you can often lead them into seeing things your way. The fastest way to do this is to do as Steven Covey said and "Seek first to understand. Then to be understood." People will listen to you once they feel like you've been listening to them.

Trust Your Gut

Your stomach is radically insightful. Think about how many times you've wanted to do something that made sense on paper, but there was an uncomfortable rumbling in your gut. I've been wrong more times than I can count. My gut, however, has a flawless record. The biggest mistakes of my life have been made in direct contradiction to what it told me to do.

You have the opportunity to trust your instincts – use it. Cleaning up after our mistakes is an unfortunate part of life and business, but cleaning up after mistakes we knew better than to make is much more painful and all too often requires a lawyer to finish handling the details.

Your stomach is often your subconscious trying to tell you something that you're too blind to consciously know. Ignoring it can lead to a broken heart and a busted bank account.

"I rely far more on gut instincts than researching huge amounts of statistics."

—*Sir Richard Branson*

CHAPTER SEVEN
Transform Your Life

If you've been thinking about a change for a while but haven't yet acted upon it, you're not alone. And it's not your fault. Many people resist change and endure the life they have, as unsatisfying as it may be. They may not feel the driving impulse to turn things around until the situation and their misery become almost unbearable. That's when some give up hope, but the pain is what motivates us to greatness! Desperation can be a wonderful motivator for change. Control it and make it work for you.

As Janis Joplin sang, 'Freedom's just another word for nothing left to lose.' When you're at a point where you feel you have nothing left, that's a powerful place. After all, it's easy to bet the ranch when you don't own it. Harness that feeling and channel it toward positive change. It's the same with all negative emotions. Either use them as catalysts to create your own destiny or be destined to stay in that state of anger, unhappiness, misery, and desperation.

You have the power within you to make any change you want. Transformation is in your hands.

The Hindsight Principle

You have the opportunity to change your life at any time. Evaluate where you are now – business choices, relationships, anything you're in the middle of – and ask yourself, "If I had known then what I know now, would I have pursued this?" If the answer is, "No, I never would have started," then it's time to change it or try something new.

While it's difficult to think of losing what you've worked hard to build up in both your professional and personal life, understand that it's probably not going to get much better if things stay the way they are. Einstein said that the definition of insanity is doing the same thing over and over and expecting a different result. Shift the paradigm. Create a new life – one that you really want and deserve. Stop taking dictation from everyone around you.

Maintaining Momentum

You don't have to settle for what you've got. Don't stop at good when you can have great! That goes for business, sex, anything! The best way to keep momentum is by building on the successes you already have. Every single day, reevaluate where you are and where you want to be. Many people set goals, then put them aside or forget about them. That's easy to do, especially once you're comfortable, but that will never get you where you deserve to be. If you want your business to thrive, you've got to up the intensity every day and follow up on the opportunities you have. Pay attention to every part of your business – they all contribute to your bottom line – and focus on doing the most productive thing every moment of every day.

The same thing applies to personal relationships. When two people first start dating, they constantly do wonderful, sweet, nurturing things for each other. But as the relationship becomes more familiar and secure, that often stops. Once you've won someone over, though, your work isn't done. Taking your partner for granted only makes them feel less special and creates dissatisfaction and insecurity, shaking the ground of your 'stable 'relationship. Don't just be satisfied with what you have – work on making it even better.

Daily reminding yourself and your partner how much you care. Plan ways to make your love feel special. Then you'll always be on track, focusing on the positive aspects of the relationship and the endless possibilities! This also sends a clear message to Your Great Within. You're reminding yourself of your love and devotion to this special person.

*"There is no point at which you can say, 'Well,
I'm successful now; I might as well take a
nap.'"*

—*Carrie Fisher*

Reinvention

Life gives us many opportunities to reinvent ourselves. So does failure. If a career or relationship didn't work out for you, it probably wasn't a good fit. Now is the time to design your new life. The pen is in your hand. The fire is in your soul.

> *I have not failed. I've just found 10,000 ways that won't work.*
>
> —*Thomas Edison*

From The Heart

None of the strategies in the book will work if they don't come from heart. Your passion will take you places your intellect can't envision. Don't lose a minute. Time doesn't tolerate indecision. Tomorrow, you'll be another day older and either closer or further away from your Dream World. Seize every moment of every day. Love and Dream with all your soul. We have it in us to love deeply and that's the only love that can set us free.

Thank you so much for your desire to empower your life. In a world where mediocrity seems to be acceptable, we need leaders and visionaries now more than ever.

Please connect with me on social media - the links are in the intro of this book. Better yet, come see me at one of my seminars. It would be an honor to thank you in person.

May your life be filled with love, prosperity, and bliss. I honor you for the time you've devoted to empowering yourself and I'm honored to be your partner in this amazing journey. You and you alone hold the power to having anything you want in life! Dare to Live.

Traci's Famous 7% Sales Script

Give yourself a raise!

As a Realtor, we set our own value. For much of my career, I earned 7% on my listings. And my clients were usually money ahead by paying a premium commission. You can download a free copy at www.Www.MillionaireMindsetCoaches.com/resources.
Feel free to change the 7% to whatever commission seems like a win - win in your market.

There are countless ways to earn more in your real estate business - selling more homes is rarely the best option!

Give yourself a raise! How to get 7 Percent listings
* Show your value first
* Address it before it comes up.
Learn this script word for word. If it doesn't role off your tongue you're gonna strike out.

Remember some of the highest paid people on earth follow a script or memorize a play book. Brad Pitt didn't ad lib his role in Fight Club.
As soon as I was done with my listing presentation this is my next statement:

One question that often comes up with sellers who have done their home work is what are my fees. Mr. And Mrs. Seller, I work for you - so that s your decision. We can do 6 or 7 percent. My sellers who are themselves successful sales people will almost always opt for the 7 percent. May I show you how you just might put more money in your pocket by offering a very competitive brokerage fee?
As you know, most of us Realtors are strictly commission. So doesn t it make sense that the best agents want to maximize their time?

Well, Mr. And Mrs. Seller, did you know that the commission offered is right on the MLS sheet? (point it out and circle it). Do you think it s possible that perhaps agents might notice that when they are deciding which homes to show?

So let s say an agent has set up several showing in your subdivision. And they are running late and only have time to show one more, but they have 3 scheduled - all of which meet the needs wants and desires of their buyer. Is it possible that an agent might consider showing the home with a higher commission first? I m not saying it right or it s wrong - just that it's often human nature, don't you agree? I just know that there is a reason that builders often offer huge bonuses to agents. Because it works. Just like it works in every other industry. Ever been out for margaritas and the waitress suggested a tequila you ve never heard of? Well, it s possible that that tequila maker is running an incentive to the waiter that sells the most of their brand.

Mr. And Mrs. Seller, what do you say we start out at the 7%. And if we don t hit a home run and have to do a price adjustment down the road we can always reduce the brokerage fees. Doesn t that seem reasonable?

With Gratitude

We get what we Think about and Thank about.

I'm flooded with gratitude for the many folks who have loved and supported me on this amazing journey.

SuperDave Gagnon, your love has set me free, and I adore you and love you with all my soul. Your kindness, benevolence, and love personifies Grace and Strength. I'm so very blessed to be in Your Heart and in your Cart (you golfers know what I mean).

Thank you, Geno and Gebo Gero, my beautiful parents. Your love was the foundation for everything good and beautiful in my life. Thank you for rescuing me as a three-day-old baby and for showing me the true power of Love.

Thank you to the 6,000 plus agents in my eXp family! Your leadership and commitment to each other's success is inspiring and motivating. I'm honored to serve you all.

Glenn Sanford, thank you for creating this life-changing company. You have created a system where Realtors can get free, and grow and prosper. You are, by far, the most brilliant man I've ever met and you have forever changed the Real Estate Industry.

Pat, Angel and Bob Hays, your partnership and friendship created the power and momentum for the growth of eXp in our team. And you all truly personify a beautiful family. Y'all inspire me in every way and I'm so very grateful for your leadership.

To Tom and Marisa Truong
What an honor to be y'all's partner. You are the Great America Success Story and have helped so many Realtors grow and prosper. Your friendship is a blessing.

To Grace Walker, who has given me some of the best advice ever – from the 'Hula Hoop 'for my golf game to sage advice in my love life. I'm blessed and honored to be your friend.

To Karen Embs, who is my guiding light and my super fun friend! You personify Love and Light and Joy. I love and adore you pretty lady.

To Lenore Gregson, you personify benevolence and true Texas charm. You have helped so many people raise their image of themselves and live a happier and healthier life. Thank you for being such a wonderful friend.

Sebrina and Gene – wow – y'all have introduced us to a totally new way of living a life by design. Y'all's love and connection is inspiring in every way.

To Lynnie, who taught me so much about designing my life. You have transformed my home into the most magnificent place on earth and transformed my heart in an even more powerful way. Thank you for your beautiful friendship.

To Grace Hernandez and Chris Rebosura, my amazing partners. Your leadership and ingenuity has helped thousands of Realtors grow and prosper.

To Skip Wiley – thank you for being my Realtor when I moved to Florida and an amazing partner. I have learned more from you than words can say, and you personify strength and professionalism. Most of all, thank you for being such an amazing friend.

To Cassie, Olivia, Ellarie, and Keegan. Y'all are such a blessing to SuperDave and me. Cassie, you are the kind of Mom we all wish we'd had.

Thank you, Tony Robbins, my mentor. Your book, *Awaken the Giant Within*, was my catalyst for change. I'm honored to be one of your Platinum Partners and your guidance has been a driving force in my happiness and success. Thank you for showing the world the Power of living in a "Beautiful State."

About the Author

Traci was born in the middle of the Mojave Desert and was adopted three days later. We think that explains a lot.

Traci gets it.
She's been a successful Realtor, and she's looked like a successful Realtor, while her home was in foreclosure.

She's made millions.
And lost it all.

She's been deeply in love. And lost. And started over.

She understands the daily struggles that all Realtors face.
And she understands how to set them free.

Growing up, Traci's living room faced a laundromat. In the words of Reba McIntire, "To say the least, we were hard pressed."

She got a full ride to Baylor where she studied Education, because, apparently, she enjoyed being poor.

After five years as a teacher, she went into Real Estate and found her passion.

She went on to own the fourth-largest Century 21 office in the US – and sold it weeks before the crash in 2007. She also led the #1 Century 21 team in the nation for many years.

Traci was 'recruiter of the year 'globally for Keller Williams in 2012 and was one of the top luxury agents in San Antonio for many years.

She joined eXp in 2015 when there were less than 900 agents globally. She now has over 6,000 agents in her revenue share organization. The massive success of her inspiring partners has made her one of the top earners in the company.

Currently, Traci devotes her time to freeing Realtors from the hamster wheel and helping them get Financially Free by Mastering their Mindset.

Traci lives with her future husband, SuperDave Gagnon, and their five-pound Yorke-Poo, ShadowBox, in Hammock Beach, Florida and Manchester, New Hampshire. She works to support her golf habit. And buy puppy treats.

She's written several books and training courses and has been featured extensively on TV, radio and podcasts all over the world.

Join our private Facebook group Millionaire Mindset for Real Estate Wealth

Learn more at www.MakeFriendsWealthy.com

About the Cover

The cover is a work of Art by the ground breaking Artist, Kre8. His work is featured in some of the most exclusive art collections in the world. He is driven by passion and completely compelled to Kre8 - making history, one painting at a time. Follow him on Instagram - kre8artafax and learn more at http://www.kre8artafax.com

Made in the USA
Las Vegas, NV
11 August 2021

27980859R00037